P9-BID-613

One Hundred and Fifty

Need-to-Know

Bible
Facts

One Hundred and Fifty

Need-to-Know

Bible
Facts

Key Truths for Better Living

ED STRAUSS

BARBOUR
PUBLISHING

© 2011 by Barbour Publishing, Inc.

ISBN 978-1-61626-213-6

All rights reserved. No part of this publication may be reproduced
or transmitted for commercial purposes, except for brief quotations
in printed reviews, without written permission of the publisher.

Churches and other noncommercial interests may reproduce
portions of this book without the express written permission
of Barbour Publishing, provided that the text does not exceed
500 words and that the text is not material quoted from another
publisher. When reproducing text from this book, include the
following credit line: "From *150 Need-to-Know Bible Facts*, published by
Barbour Publishing, Inc. Used by permission."

Scripture taken from the New King James Version®. Copyright
© 1982 by Thomas Nelson, Inc. Used by permission. All rights
reserved.

Published by Barbour Publishing, Inc., P.O. Box 719, Uhrichsville,
Ohio 44683 www.barbourbooks.com

*Our mission is to publish and distribute inspirational products offering
exceptional value and biblical encouragement to the masses.*

Member of the
Evangelical Christian
Publishers Association

Printed in the United States of America.

INTRODUCTION

You've probably already noticed—the Bible is a very large and complex book.

Actually, the Bible is a compilation of 66 "books," including histories, song collections, theological treatises, and personal letters. Written by some forty writers over hundreds of years, the Bible contains 1,189 chapters, more than 31,000 verses, and upwards of 780,000 words.

So how are we to make sense of it all? *150 Need-to-Know Bible Facts* can help.

This little book takes the great themes of the Bible and distills them into quick, easy-to-read entries to give you a bird's-eye view of scripture. Though every detail of the Bible is there for a reason, you'll probably find it most helpful to understand facts like

- God created everything.
- Sin is destructive.
- We are very important to God.
- Jesus' teachings are very simple.
- Faith can conquer fear.

These "need-to-know facts"—and 145 others like them—will walk you through the biggest, most important ideas of the Bible. You'll see the big picture, not only the individual brush strokes.

We hope *150 Need-to-Know Bible Facts* will help you better understand the Bible—and better know the God who gave it to us.

THE EDITORS

1

God created *everything*.

In the beginning God created the heavens and the earth.
GENESIS 1:1

Look around you—where did everything come from? Sure, light came from the sun. . .trees grew from seeds. . .people were born to their mothers. But where did all those things originate *ultimately*? How did the sun take its place in the sky? Where did the very first seed-producing tree come from? How did your great, great, great (and so on) grandmother start the line of people that produced you?

Genesis 1 answers very simply: *God* made everything.

2

God simply *spoke* things into existence.

*Then God said, "Let there be light";
and there was light.*
GENESIS 1:3

Talented people make useful and beautiful things that enhance our lives—the houses we live in, the foods we eat, the art we enjoy. But every artisan must begin with some kind of raw material—wood, stone, grain, pigments. Not so with God.

When God wanted to create our incredible universe, He simply said the word—and it happened. Light, sky, dry land, plants, and animals. . .all arose at the command of the one true God. It's just one example of His amazing power.

3

In the beginning, the world was perfect.

Then God saw everything that He had made, and indeed it was very good.
GENESIS 1:31

The Garden of Eden was an astonishingly beautiful paradise, but Eden was just part of the Big Picture. *All* of Creation on the entire planet was "very good." All flora and fauna were flawless.

Our planet today is far from perfect. We live in a fallen world. Disease and death, thorns and thistles have overtaken paradise. And yet, pause for a moment, and you will still see so much beauty shining through that it will take your breath away.

4

The devil caused doubt and dissatisfaction.

When the woman saw that the tree was. . .desirable to make one wise, she took of its fruit and ate.
GENESIS 3:6

Adam and Eve were living in Eden. They didn't have a problem or a care. They should have been perfectly content, and they were—that is, until the devil lied and "explained" that God had deceived them in order to withhold the *best* from them. If they ate the forbidden fruit, the serpent insisted, they would be wise like God.

The only way to believe the devil was to disbelieve God—and that's what Eve did. People have been falling for that same trick ever since.

5

Sin is destructive.

For the wages of sin is death.
ROMANS 6:23

Adam and Eve's innocence was shattered the instant they disobeyed God. The sweet taste of the forbidden fruit was still on their tongues when its poison began its deadly work, quicker than a serpent's venom. Their minds were darkened, and they began seeing everything from a skewed, selfish perspective.

Worst of all, they died spiritually that day and began to die physically as well. The wages that their sin paid them was death.

Thankfully, God had already planned an antidote to the devil's poison.

6

Sin separates humanity from God.

Your iniquities have separated you from your God;
and your sins have hidden His face from you.
ISAIAH 59:2

Disobeying God came with a huge price: Humanity's relationship with the divine was sundered. To this very day, mankind's iniquity separates us from God. We can no longer see His face. "We grope for the wall like the blind" (Isaiah 59:10).

When we have no relationship with the Lord, when the power lines are down, when doubt, denial, and disobedience leave us in darkness, how can we communicate with God? We can't.

Thankfully, God had already planned a way to turn the lights back on.

7

Man at his best is insignificant.

Behold, the nations are as a drop in a bucket,
and are counted as the small dust on the scales.
ISAIAH 40:15

We pride ourselves that we've come a long way. And we have. As magnificent as mankind's civilizations of the past were, think of the astonishing technologies of the modern world.

But none of our accomplishments can *begin* to compare to the eternal, omniscient God who created the vast universe, started every swirling galaxy turning, and said to every distant, giant star, "Be!"

The Bible pegs us accurately: our greatest nations are dust specks, and we're like microbes living on them.

8

We are very important to God.

What is man that You are mindful of him,
and the son of man that You visit him?
PSALM 8:4

Since God is the infinite Creator, who are *we* that He would care about us? Why would God even give humans a second thought—particularly since we rebelled against Him?

It is precisely because God *is* infinite that He can watch a distant asteroid, yet still notice when a hair from our head falls to the ground on Earth. It is precisely because God *is* our Creator that He loves us—even in our fallen state.

And He has a wonderful plan for us.

9

The blood of sacrifices covered sin.

"The life of the flesh is in the blood, and I have given it to you upon the altar to make atonement for your souls."
LEVITICUS 17:11

The punishment for sin is death, so when someone sinned, legally, their blood had to be spilled. God allowed a substitute, however. He ordained that His people sacrifice an animal to atone for their sin. The Hebrew word for *atonement* means "to cover." In a real spiritual sense, the blood of the lamb or goat covered over a person's sin.

Every time someone sinned, however, they had to make another sacrifice. . .and another. . . and another. Clearly, this was only a temporary solution.

10

No one fully obeyed the Law of Moses.

Whoever shall keep the whole law,
and yet stumble in one point, he is guilty of all.
JAMES 2:10

To help people stay in loving relationship with Him and others, God gave them the Law of Moses. This law contained (according to the rabbis' count) 613 commandments—and people had to obey them *all*. It wasn't enough to keep the command, "You shall not commit adultery," but disobey, "You shall not gossip."

But people are only human, and the best of us trip up. (Try giving generously and cheerfully to someone whom you know won't repay.) As a result, no one kept the law perfectly.

11

God had a solution to sin.

God sent forth His Son. . .
to redeem those who were under the law.
GALATIANS 4:4–5

God was aware that even good-hearted, sincere people couldn't obey the law without fail—and that those who tried *hardest* to be righteous were often, well, self-righteous legalists. God was as displeased with merciless, unloving "righteousness" as He was with thoughtless, unloving sin.

For their part, the common people (whom the religious called "sinners") were aware of their failings, yet weary of trying to live up to impossible-to-keep standards.

The time was right, so God sent Jesus into the world with mercy and truth.

12

Jesus' life is a fact of history.

*We did not follow cunningly devised fables when we made
known to you the power and coming of our Lord Jesus
Christ, but were eyewitnesses.*
2 PETER 1:16

The Gospels tell the facts of Jesus' birth,
life, death, and resurrection. These aren't
made-up fables like the insane adventures of
the Greek gods. No, the powerful miracles the
apostles describe actually happened! Peter, John,
and Matthew were eyewitnesses.

In addition, tens of thousands of people from
one end of Israel to the other had met Jesus and
seen His miracles. As Paul pointed out, "This
thing was not done in a corner" (Acts 26:26).

Make no mistake: the four Gospels are
accurate historical reports.

13

Jesus is a perfect representation of God.

He is the image of the invisible God.
COLOSSIANS 1:15

The Bible *tells* us that God has great love for us, but He knew we were all basically from Missouri: We needed to be *shown*. So God sent His only Son to Earth to demonstrate what His love was like.

Jesus was the perfect representation of God, and He empathized with us and put up with everything we endure: hunger, thirst, weariness, and temptation. By living among us, by caring for us—then giving His very life—Jesus showed us that God indeed loved us.

14

Jesus' blood completely cleanses us.

Jesus Christ. . .loved us and washed us
from our sins in His own blood.
REVELATION 1:5

When John the Baptist saw Jesus he shouted, "Behold! The Lamb of God who takes away the sin of the world!" (John 1:29). He was right: Jesus was the final, perfect sacrificial lamb, who offered His own lifeblood to save us.

Jesus' blood didn't just temporarily *cover* our sin like the blood of sacrificial lambs had done. Jesus took our iniquities completely away. His blood *washed away* our sins, leaving us clean. And He did it *one* time, once and for all.

15

There's infallible proof that Jesus lives!

He also presented Himself alive after
His suffering by many infallible proofs.
ACTS 1:3

When Jesus appeared to His disciples after rising from the dead, they recognized Him all right, but thought they were seeing His ghost. So Jesus offered His disciples proof that it was really *Him*: He ate food and told them, "Touch Me."

That convinced them!

For the next forty days, before He ascended to heaven, Jesus appeared to over five hundred people and offered *many* and *infallible* proofs that He had indeed been resurrected from the dead. He wanted us to know that fact beyond all doubt.

16

Women were the first witnesses.

When He rose early on the first day of the week,
He appeared first to Mary Magdalene.
MARK 16:9

Two thousand years ago, Jewish religious leaders had a low opinion of women. Their testimony wasn't even accepted in a court of law; only male witnesses were believed. Yet all four Gospels report that *women* were the first to see Jesus alive again—and a formerly disreputable lady was first of all!

If the apostles had invented reports of seeing Jesus, they'd have surely claimed that one of *them* had seen Him. But the truth was what it was, so they told it like it happened.

17

The Gospels were written to inspire faith.

*These are written that you may believe
that Jesus is the Christ, the Son of God.*
JOHN 20:31

Many people think that the purpose of the Gospels is to inform us that an enlightened teacher named Jesus once walked the earth and advised us to love one another and do good—or that His miracles proved that He was some kind of holy man.

That's missing the main point by a country mile. John puts it succinctly: the *main* reason the Gospels were written was to cause us to believe that Jesus is God's Son—the only one who can give us eternal life.

18

God loved us at our worst.

*God demonstrates His own love toward us, in that while
we were still sinners, Christ died for us.*
ROMANS 5:8

Many of us secretly suspect that God only
loves "good people" who've already got
something going—and are already doing their
best to love and obey Him. That's an easy mistake
to slip into, but it *is* a mistake. God loves people
who are still wallowing in sin, hurting themselves
and others, and insisting that they don't even
need God.

God sent His Son, Jesus, to make the ultimate
sacrifice when we were totally undeserving and
unappreciative of His immense love.

19

Our sin is utterly gone.

You will cast all our sins into the depths of the sea.
MICAH 7:19

Once you're forgiven, God doesn't hang on to a ledger listing your sins, pull it out every time you trip up, tap His fingers and say, "Just to let you know, I haven't forgotten these things." No. He says He has cast your sins—*all* your sins—into the Abyss, the deepest trench in the profoundest depths of the ocean, sunk to the utter bottom, never to be recovered.

Once your sins are forgiven, they are gone indeed, and you are forgiven indeed.

20

God has adopted us.

You received the Spirit of adoption by
whom we cry out, "Abba, Father."
ROMANS 8:15

We weren't God's sons and daughters to start
with. We were like street urchins, grimy
with sin, all our unrighteousness like filthy rags
draped around us, homeless, destitute waifs. . .but
then. . .

God adopted us as His own children, washed
us clean, dressed us in robes of righteousness,
and gave us the immense privilege of calling Him
Father. We have been adopted into His family and
warmly invited to sit at the royal table.

Oh, there are a few house rules. . .but we'll
get to those.

21

Jesus literally lives in your heart.

God has sent forth the Spirit of His Son into your hearts.
GALATIANS 4:6

When you put your faith in Jesus Christ and ask Him to save you, His Spirit enters your heart—literally. This isn't just a figure of speech. God sends the Spirit of Jesus into your very being and He takes up residence there. He says, "I will dwell in them" (2 Corinthians 6:16).

You may argue that you're not "holy" enough for God to live in, that you're too much of a mess. But that's precisely why Jesus enters your life—to *make* you holy.

22

Only Jesus can save us.

Jesus said to him, "I am the way, the truth, and the life.
No one comes to the Father except through Me."
JOHN 14:6

We should respect other peoples' beliefs, but let's be very clear: Jesus stated that He is *the* truth, *the* life, and *the* only way to God. He is not one path among many. He is no optional side dish in the cafeteria of world beliefs.

Other religions teach *some* truth and may even lead *part*way to God, but Jesus is the only one who can save us, the only one who can get us completely across the yawning chasm of sin to the Father's arms.

23

We can now live Moses' law.

All the law is fulfilled in one word, even in this:
"You shall love your neighbor as yourself."
GALATIANS 5:14

It was a small command tucked away in a dry book of ceremonial laws. It wasn't even listed among the Ten Commandments. Yet these seven simple words in Leviticus 19:18—"You shall love your neighbor as yourself"—are the heart of the law.

The Law of Moses was strict and complicated. Jesus' message was merciful and simple: love God and love the person next to you. Do that and you just fulfilled all the requirements of the law.

Talk about keeping things simple!

24

We must love and obey God.

That you may love the LORD your God, that you may
obey His voice, and that you may cling to Him,
for He is your life.
DEUTERONOMY 30:20

Imagine that you must cross a swollen river. God can easily withstand the raging current, but all around you, you see debris being swept away. "Hold tightly to Me, My child," He says, and though you are afraid, you do. You obey His voice and cling to Him for your very life.

You must not only believe that He is strong enough to save you, but you must know that He loves you enough to actually do so. When you really "get" that, you will trust and love Him in return.

25

We must love one another.

Beloved, let us love one another, for love is of God; and everyone who loves is born of God and knows God.
1 JOHN 4:7

Jesus said to love one another—even our enemies. (That surely includes family and friends at their crankiest.)

But why must we *love* them? Really, aren't we doing enough already if we manage to ignore them or to tolerate them? Why must we actually *love* them?

We must love others because love comes from God and God now lives in our heart. We love others because we are God's child. Loving others shows that we truly know God, and know who He is: Love.

26

We love Jesus when we love others.

"Inasmuch as you did it to one of the least of these My brethren, you did it to Me."
MATTHEW 25:40

We are to show love to others by doing tangible acts of kindness, doing what we can to meet their spiritual, emotional, and physical needs. But Jesus knew that some people weren't easy or convenient to love, so He emphasized that showing kindness to even the lowest person was showing it to *Him* personally.

Jesus loves every man, woman, and child on Earth and strongly identifies with their pain, their sorrows, and their need for love. He wants us to feel that way, too.

27

We must put ourselves in others' shoes.

"Whatever you want men to do to you, do also to them."
MATTHEW 7:12

Moses' law commanded us to love our neighbor, but that raised the question, "Um. . .what am I supposed to *do* to show them love?" So Jesus turned it around and basically said, "Well think: how would you like others to treat *you*?"

The answer is: I'd like to be treated with respect, to be given the benefit of the doubt, to be helped when I need help, to be forgiven my mistakes, etc.

Well, there you have it! That's how you should treat others.

28

We must forgive others.

*"If you have anything against anyone,
forgive him, that your Father in heaven
may also forgive you your trespasses."*
MARK 11:25

We often think that if someone offends us,
we can either choose to nobly forgive him
or we can elect *not* to—that God will understand
because, after all, that person really was/is a
rotter.

Now, it often takes time to work through deep
pain before we can forgive a serious offence. God
knows that. He's helping us through that process.
What God *doesn't* have time for, however, is us
stubbornly hanging on to every trivial offence.

We ourselves need to be forgiven. Let's forgive
others.

29

We need to stretch our love.

Above all things have fervent love for one another,
for "love will cover a multitude of sins."
1 PETER 4:8

Some people mentally assent to Jesus'
command to love one another. Their love,
however, has its definite limits. It generally holds
up as long as the other person doesn't become *too*
aggravating or cross them one too many times.

Peter clarified this, saying, "Have *fervent* love
for one another." The Greek word for *fervent*
means "stretched out." This kind of longsuffering,
go-the-extra-mile love is the only kind that keeps
on forgiving when the other person bugs you
repeatedly.

30

Jesus' teachings are very simple.

I fear, lest somehow, as the serpent deceived Eve by his craftiness, so your minds may be corrupted from the simplicity that is in Christ.
2 CORINTHIANS 11:3

Paul told the Christians of Corinth to beware if anyone rolled into town preaching "another Jesus"—a Jesus who suddenly had a bunch of requirements and regulations to help them save themselves. No matter how wise and sensible it seemed, it was like the serpent showing up to deceive Eve all over again!

The real Gospel message is simple. Not necessarily easy to live but certainly easy to grasp: believe on Jesus to be saved, love God, and love your fellow man. Period.

31

Even God's "foolish" ways are wise.

The foolishness of God is wiser than men,
and the weakness of God is stronger than men.
1 CORINTHIANS 1:25

The ancient Greeks were, like many people today, intellectual and philosophical. To them, inheriting heaven by faith in a bloodied, crucified Savior was foolishness. Surely the path to higher celestial states required secret wisdom, elevating one's spirit by an esoteric process of enlightenment.

The problem was—besides being wrong—that much of their "secret wisdom" was highly convoluted mental gymnastics. God's "simple foolishness" was far wiser than the vaunted tower of intellectual cards the Greeks had erected.

32

Christianity is a sane, reasonable faith.

"I am not mad, most noble Festus,
but speak the words of truth and reason."
ACTS 26:25

Many people suspect that putting their faith in Christ involves shutting down their brain and making a blind, emotional leap of faith in denial of everything that their rational mind *would* have told them had they not chosen to turn it off. Not so.

The Christian faith is based on truth. God exists. Christianity is based on actual historical facts. It is reasonable and true. It can stand the scrutiny of rational minds and bring even scholars and scientists to their knees.

33

Jesus' resurrection is credible.

*"Why should it be thought incredible
by you that God raises the dead?"*
ACTS 26:8

That God raises the dead to eternal life did not seem incredible to Paul two thousand years ago, and it should seem even *less* so to us today. After all, scientists recently discovered that a species of jellyfish ages *backward* and is *immortal*!

Think of other "impossibilities" of God's creation: life survives without oxygen in pools of sulphuric acid, thrives in scalding sub-oceanic vents, and lives in the arid, frozen valleys of Antarctica.

That God should raise the dead to life is a miracle, yes. . .but hardly incredible.

34

Luke accurately researched his Gospel.

*It seemed good to me also, having had perfect
understanding of all things from the very first,
to write to you an orderly account.*
LUKE 1:3

How do we know that the accounts of Jesus'
life are accurate? Well, Matthew and John
were eyewitnesses. And Luke is widely admitted to
be one of the world's most trustworthy historians.
He sailed to Israel to meticulously research the
facts, interview witnesses, and write an orderly
account of what happened.

The gospels are not like those ludicrous
magazines you see at the checkout stand. The
Gospels are accurate historical reports. You can
be certain that the events of Jesus' life happened
just as recorded.

35

Christians are treasure seekers.

Search for her as for hidden treasures;
then you will understand the fear of the LORD,
and find the knowledge of God.
PROVERBS 2:4–5

You've seen those documentaries where treasure hunters spend years and use the most cutting-edge technology to search for lost treasure. Sometimes they strike pay dirt, and sometimes, well, they're still out there searching while the credits roll.

If you seek treasure in the Bible your spiritual Geiger counters will constantly be beeping and your dives will always be rewarded. Instead of finding doubloons, however, you'll be discovering wisdom for life and awesome truths about God.

36

God's Word is our spiritual food.

Your words were found, and I ate them, and Your word
was to me the joy and rejoicing of my heart.
JEREMIAH 15:16

Jesus said that man couldn't live by bread
alone, but by every word that God speaks
(Matthew 4:4).

Jeremiah said that he *ate* God's words. Of
course, he wasn't literally chewing on a scroll, but
the comparison is a good one. God's Word is our
spiritual food.

It's not enough to merely find food, or to
taste it. You must chew and digest it. That's
when it gives you energy and life. And that's
what happens when you read God's Word and
"swallow" it down into your heart.

37

God's Word gives us faith.

Faith comes by hearing, and hearing by the word of God.
ROMANS 10:17

What do we do when we need more faith? We can pray for God to give us more, just like Jesus' disciples did when they said, "Increase our faith" (Luke 17:5). However, God has already supplied a sure-fire way for us to increase faith—by hearing and reading His Word.

Just as we build and strengthen muscles by spending time exercising, we build our faith by spending time reading the Bible and meditating on it. And we must read it regularly.

38

We need to check
what the Bible says.

They received the word with all readiness, and searched the
Scriptures daily to find out whether these things were so.
ACTS 17:11

When Paul told his fellow Jews that Jesus was
their long-awaited Savior, some rejected
the claim without giving it a chance. Others
who were more fair-minded, however, listened
carefully then did their own Bible research to
check out what Paul was saying.

When someone teaches you something new,
check it out with the Bible. Dig deep and see if
it's so. They might be right and your life will be
enriched. Or you might find out that's *not* what
the Bible teaches.

Either way, check it out.

39

We don't know better than the Bible.

Behold, they have rejected the word of the LORD;
so what wisdom do they have?
JEREMIAH 8:9

Some of the world's wisest people are *not* very informed when it comes to God and the Bible. They're highly focused on their particular area of expertise, but they're novices when it comes to spiritual matters. As long as they admit their limitations, it's not a problem.

The danger comes when they suppose their intelligence makes them wiser than God's Word. But what does a degree in, say, astrophysics count for when most of the questions on the exam are about man's relationship to God?

40

The Holy Spirit helps us.

"The Holy Spirit. . .will teach you all things, and bring to your remembrance all things that I said to you."
JOHN 14:26

Jesus sent His Holy Spirit to dwell in our hearts and minds. Think of the Spirit as an all-wise, live-in tutor—a teacher who knows the answer to every question. The Spirit of God is God Himself. No wonder He can teach us "all things."

One of the most usual ways the Spirit teaches us is by reminding us of the things Jesus said. Of course, we have to first *read* Jesus' words in the Bible. Then He can bring them *back* to our memory.

41

God's Spirit gives us love.

*The love of God has been poured out in our hearts by the
Holy Spirit who was given to us.*
ROMANS 5:5

Jesus taught that the only way to fulfill the Law
of Moses was to love God with all our hearts
and to love our fellow man as much as we love
ourselves. It sounds simple, but actually *living* it is
a very tall order!

How on earth can we do that? Humanly, we
don't *have* that much love.

The solution: God gives it to us! God *is* love,
and when His Spirit fills us, He pours out the love
of God in our hearts.

42

The Holy Spirit gives us power.

*You shall receive power when the Holy Spirit has come
upon you; and you shall be witnesses to Me.*
ACTS 1:8

Perhaps you've heard the saying, "The Holy
Spirit gives us power to live the Christian
life." This is true. God wants you to live Jesus'
teachings, yet He is aware that you can't do it by
yourself. But when His Spirit empowers you, you
can.

And when people around you see true
Christianity in action, it inspires them to believe
in God. Your very life becomes a witness. The
Holy Spirit also empowers you to speak out and
tell others how Jesus has changed your life.

43

The Spirit grows virtues in us.

The fruit of the Spirit is love, joy, peace, longsuffering, kindness, goodness, faithfulness, gentleness, self-control.
GALATIANS 5:22–23

The "fruit" of the Spirit is the virtues that God grows in a Christian's life. They won't spring forth at once, fully grown. However, once the Spirit enters, they begin to grow. They are in stark contrast to natural vices such as "lewdness. . . jealousies, outbursts of wrath, selfish ambitions," etc. (Galatians 5:19–20).

This doesn't mean that if you still struggle with anger you're not saved. But it does mean that if you allow God to change you, your virtues will replace your vices.

44

Jesus' mother gave good advice.

His mother said to the servants,
"Whatever He says to you, do it."
JOHN 2:5

When Mary and Jesus were at a marriage in Cana, the host ran out of wine. Mary turned to the servants and said, "Whatever He says to you, do it." Jesus then told them to fill up the water jugs. They obeyed, and He turned the water into wine.

This command sums up our Christian duty. Sometimes, what Jesus tells us to do makes little sense at first. Sometimes He commands us to do something difficult. But if He says to do it, we should *do* it.

45

Obeying Jesus proves we love Him.

"If you love Me, keep My commandments."
JOHN 14:15

Christians are to love Jesus. And how do we know if we *actually* love Him? Because we have warm feelings when we think about Him? Well, that's a good start. But contrary to songs on the radio, true love is not just emotions or an endorphin rush.

When you truly love someone, you're willing to do anything for them. When they ask you a favor, why, you roll up your sleeves.

Jesus said, "Keep My commandments." So let's put our love into action.

46

We must lose our lives for Jesus.

"He who finds his life will lose it, and he who loses his life for My sake will find it."
MATTHEW 10:39

Many people seek the things of this life first and foremost. They focus on the material goods and the pleasures of this world, and though they may *get* a comfortable life, they lose something infinitely more valuable in the process—their spiritual life.

Christians may seem to "lose out" by making sacrifices because they're determined to put Jesus first and love others. But in reality, by living unselfishly, they *find* life in all its fullness—both in this world and in the world to come.

47

We must be nonconformists.

Do not be conformed to this world, but be transformed
by the renewing of your mind.
ROMANS 12:2

Many of us like to think that we're nonconformists, but often we're as caught up in the lemming mentality as the person next to us. We find ourselves subscribing to the lifestyle and mind-set and blogs of one crowd or another.

The pull of the world is so strong that it's an ongoing struggle to avoid being sucked into it. The best way is to let God's Spirit transform us. He does that by renewing our minds while we're reading the Bible and praying.

48

Sins of omission are sins.

Therefore, to him who knows to do good
and does not do it, to him it is sin.
JAMES 4:17

Hurting others—whether willfully or through a lack of concern—is wrong. We all know that. But there are sins of omission as well as sins of commission. Is there a lonely shut-in you've been avoiding visiting? An act of kindness you've been meaning to do? A blank on the volunteer list where your name would fit nicely?

Failure to do small things seems almost too insignificant to count as sins—but they *are* sins. Do something on God's "To Do" list today.

49

We will reap what we sow.

Whatever a man sows, that he will also reap.
GALATIANS 6:7

Many people, when something bad happens,
chalk it up to so-called karma, "cause and
effect." Nonsense. The principle of "you reap
what you sow" comes straight from the Bible.

Paul is speaking here about eternity: if we
sow to the Spirit, we'll reap everlasting life. But
this principle surely applies to things in this life
also. Selfish, unloving actions—unless we repent
of them—have a way of coming back to us. But
the happy news is this: whatever good we do will
return to bless us.

50

We must allow God to prune us.

"Every branch in Me that. . .bears fruit He prunes,
that it may bear more fruit."
JOHN 15:2

Jesus compared Himself to a grapevine and us to individual branches. When we're joined to Jesus, we bear good fruit—Christian virtues, good deeds, and a life that's a witness to others.

If any branch is dead, God simply lops the whole thing off. But if any parts of a *living* branch are using up sap but not bearing fruit, He pulls out His pruning shears and snips those suckers off.

We need to allow God to cut sins and bad habits out of our life.

51

We must get rid of our garbage.

Turn away my eyes from looking at worthless things,
and revive me in Your way.
PSALM 119:37

Here's a guy who was honest enough to admit that he lacked the willpower to turn his eyes away from desiring worthless things. So he asked God to help him. Another thing: he was *trying* to walk in God's path, but he'd been fumbling recently.

"Revive me! Give me a personal revival!" That's a prayer that we all do well to pray. And revival often begins with a sincere desir to bag up the garbage in our lives and put it out on the curb.

52

God searches our hearts.

Search me, O God. . .and see if there is any wicked
way in me, and lead me in the way everlasting.
PSALM 139:23–24

When we pray this prayer, we open up all our doors and dresser drawers and give God permission to go through and search out any sins. Mind you, God *already* knows us well. But this invites Him to bring these sins to our attention and have a heart-to-heart chat about them.

God doesn't do this to make us despair at how bad we are, but because He loves us. He wants to get rid of anything that hinders us from walking "in the way everlasting."

53

Living in love is being full of God.

You, being rooted and grounded in love. . .
may be filled with all the fullness of God.
EPHESIANS 3:17, 19

We all wish for more of God's presence in our life, but secretly fear it. We suspect that experiencing God fully only happens to missionaries in foreign lands—which we are not—or to wide-eyed fanatics—which we'd rather avoid.

But the truth is more ordinary and closer to home: We are to live a life filled with love. We must send our roots deep down into love and build on it as a foundation. It's a lifelong process, but we can begin today.

54

Living God's Word frees us.

"If you abide in My word. . .you shall know the truth,
and the truth shall make you free."
JOHN 8:31–32

We're familiar with the saying, "The truth shall make you free," and apply it to a number of things. Indeed, knowing the truth about a situation in your childhood, or *who* said what to whom yesterday, can be liberating. . .or at least a relief.

But if you want to be truly liberated, you must get your head around what Jesus was saying: only knowing and living *His* words will actually set you free. And you must *abide in*—continue living—the truths Jesus taught.

55

God commands us not to gossip.

"You shall not go about as a talebearer among your people."
LEVITICUS 19:16

God made us social creatures who need to
share what's happening in our lives and
families, and to catch up on the news about
others. Yet He commands us not to gossip—
spread tales about others—even if they're *true*
tales.

How can we avoid crossing the line from
chatting to gossiping? Well, if we love the person
we're talking about, we'll use more discretion
when deciding how much, if anything, we say.
And while *some* people need to know the details,
not everybody does.

56

God commands us to be honest.

These are the things you shall do:
Speak each man the truth to his neighbor.
ZECHARIAH 8:16

We expect others to be honest with us in everyday dealings. We deeply admire those who are honest when honesty costs them or is embarrassing. After all, we ourselves sometimes struggle whether to 'fess up or not.

But "honesty is the best policy," as they say.

Honesty is not just the *best* policy, however. It's literally a commandment. Exodus 20:16 tells us to not bear witness against our neighbor. That's one of the ten "you shall *nots.*" This is one of the "you shall *do*" commands.

57

Shortchanging others is stealing.

"You shall not cheat your neighbor, nor rob him."
LEVITICUS 19:13

We're appalled at the thought of breaking into our neighbor's house and robbing him—which is a fortunate thing. But we shouldn't cheat or shortchange our neighbors either. (And remember: everyone is our neighbor.)

That means, for example, that we shouldn't take advantage of anyone's ignorance and sell them an overrated product or dump damaged goods on them. If we're selling a used car that has problems, we should disclose those problems.

We wouldn't sell a bum steer to Jesus, so we shouldn't do it to others.

58

We must return lost items.

*"If you meet your enemy's ox or his donkey going astray,
you shall surely bring it back to him again."*
EXODUS 23:4

You get a rush out of returning lost items to
those you *love*, right? You smile broadly as
you hand it over, thoroughly enjoying their relief
and profuse thanks. It feels good!

But when it comes to strangers, we're
sometimes tempted to apply the saying, "Finders
keepers, losers weepers." Or when it comes to
those who hate us, we might even feel a twinge of
pleasure as we let their donkey amble by.

Don't. God says go out of your way to return
it.

59

We should be kind and affectionate.

Be kindly affectionate to one another with brotherly love, in honor giving preference to one another.
ROMANS 12:10

It's one thing to say, "Love one another." It's really closing all the loopholes to say, "Be *kindly affectionate* to one another." Otherwise you'd *love* quite a few people but not particularly like them. To be "kindly affectionate," however, implies that you actually *like* loving them.

As if that weren't enough, this verse takes everything one step further: you are to honor fellow believers—treat even the lowliest with respect. When you do that, you end up being kind and affectionate to everyone.

60

Christians should be united.

That you all speak the same thing,
and that there be no divisions among you. . . .
1 CORINTHIANS 1:10

Verses like this have been used to argue that
unity consists of everyone, like one giant
chorus, all speaking the exact same thing on every
issue. This is not unity but mere conformity. The
humorous catch is that churches who demand
such "unity" believe that *they* have it right and
everyone should agree with *them*.

We should definitely "speak the same
thing" on the basic tenets of the faith. However,
Christian charity dictates that we not despise
fellow believers who disagree on secondary issues.

61

God wants us to attend church.

Let us consider one another in order to stir up love and good works, not forsaking the assembling of ourselves together.
HEBREWS 10:24–25

There are many good reasons to attend church faithfully. For one, there is beauty and power in united worship. For another, the pastor might motivate you with a good message. And then there's the chance to admire the sea of colorful Easter bonnets.

Seriously. . .attending church is also a great time to connect with fellow believers, to encourage one another, to pray for one another, and to stir each other up to live as Christians. You attend church not just for yourself but for others, too.

62

Shameless self-promotion backfires.

It is not good to eat much honey;
so to seek one's own glory is not glory.
PROVERBS 25:27

Why isn't it good to eat too much honey? Well, it seems great at first—like any very rich dessert—but as Proverbs 25:16 says, the person who eats a whole lot of honey ends up *sick* of it.

It's the same thing with someone who constantly tries to attract attention and get people to admire them—they get a reputation as a braggart and a show-off.

There's nothing wrong with sincere praise. Just don't go out of your way to *seek* it.

63

Mere knowledge can bloat us.

We know that we all have knowledge.
Knowledge puffs up, but love edifies.
1 CORINTHIANS 8:1

As Christians, we should study the Bible and seek to grow in the faith—but growing spiritually is not the same thing as memorizing Bible trivia and packing away knowledge. Merely filling our head with facts will bloat our ego into some unnatural shape—*puff* us up. But having love will edify us—*build* us up.

Bible facts and trivia can be interesting and fun, but if we are to be built solidly to last, let's grow in love for God and others.

64

We must avoid conceit.

*Do not set your mind on high things, but associate with
the humble. Do not be wise in your own opinion.*
ROMANS 12:16

Ah yes, conceit. We're all prone to it in certain
areas. We have lofty opinions of ourselves
and high expectations of what we'll do. We're
convinced that we're wise and we speak our
opinions with confidence, certain that we're right.

Pride is a common human vice. That's why
the Bible cautions us to not be self-absorbed, nor
to admire our own wisdom, but to come down
and rub shoulders with humble, ordinary people.

After all, we're really rather ordinary
ourselves.

65

We should desire to be great.

*"Whoever desires to become great among you
shall be your servant."*
MARK 10:43

There's nothing wrong with desiring to be
great—as long as it's true greatness one
desires. True greatness means humbly serving
others, because one esteems others to be better
than himself (Philippians 2:3). When someone
has that attitude, they've attained greatness.

Those who are great in God's eyes don't *think*
that they're so hot. They're very aware of their
weaknesses and failings. It's not that they have an
inferiority complex; they've simply taken a sober
look at themselves.

We should desire that kind of greatness.

66

We can do nothing of ourselves.

"I am the vine, you are the branches.
He who abides in Me, and I in him, bears much fruit;
for without Me you can do nothing."
JOHN 15:5

Jesus said, "Without Me you can do *nothing*," yet ungodly people often do well in this life—they build successful businesses and own nice houses and cars. Jesus was saying, however, that unless we're joined to Him, we have zero hope of eternal life. The sap of His Spirit in us causes us to bear "fruit"—virtues, good works, etc.—but we can't do that on our own.

People *can* be successful in this brief life, true, but if they're not alive spiritually, they and all that they do amounts to nothing.

67

It's best to get angry slowly.

Let every man be swift to hear,
slow to speak, slow to wrath.
JAMES 1:19

If you have a quick temper, you might be thinking, "*Right*. 'Be slow to wrath.' If only it were that easy." Well, it may not be easy, but it can be done.

James *first* says to do two things to throw a wet blanket on a hot temper: first, be quick to hear the other person out. Don't jump to conclusions. Second: be slow to speak. Bite your tongue. Don't engage your mouth too quickly.

James's tips are guaranteed to slow down a quick temper.

68

Arguing is often utterly pointless.

How forceful are right words!
But what does your arguing prove?
JOB 6:25

There's no arguing the fact that reasonable words are more effective than pointless arguing. (Well, a person could dispute that, but they'd only be proving its point.)

Disagreements are to be expected, but too often they develop into emotional exchanges. Tempers flare, voices are raised, and the only thing anyone manages to prove is that two people are talking and, apparently, no longer listening.

We mistakenly feel that heated arguments are "forceful." But surprise! They're really not. Gently spoken reasons are what truly convince people.

69

God hates evil thoughts.

"Let none of you think evil in your heart against your neighbor. . . . For all these are things that I hate," says the LORD.

ZECHARIAH 8:17

There are valid reasons to be angry, but Jesus surprised a lot of people by saying that if they were angry at a person without a cause they'd be judged as if they'd committed murder. If they lusted they were already guilty of adultery (Matthew 5:21–30).

They shouldn't have been surprised. God has *always* been concerned with the quality of our brain waves. After all, murders begin with angry intentions, and adultery begins with silent lust. Stop the evil thoughts and the evil deeds won't happen.

70

Don't seek revenge.

See that no one renders evil for evil to anyone,
but always pursue what is good.
1 THESSALONIANS 5:15

We understand about not paying back evil to someone who has done evil to us because evil is, well, evil. And Christians don't do evil. But any kind of revenge, however petty, is bad. (You couldn't call it "pursuing good," could you?)

Solomon said, "Do not say, 'I will do to him just as he has done to me' " (Proverbs 24:29). That means that even "getting even" or "tit for tat" is out.

Let's do what the Bible *says*: Let's do what is *good* in return.

71

Getting even messes things up.

Do not avenge yourselves. . .for it is written,
"Vengeance is Mine, I will repay," says the Lord.
ROMANS 12:19

Why *shouldn't* we get back at those who wrong
us? Well, God wants us to love others in
the hope that they'll repent and change. . .but
us getting revenge on them shows them we hate
them and haven't forgiven them. When we hurt
them in return, they get our message loud and
clear.

Let's not send the wrong message.

If love and kindness doesn't wake them up,
but they keep on offending, be sure that God will
eventually take vengeance on them.

72

Gloating over your enemy is self-defeating.

Do not rejoice when your enemy falls. . .
lest the LORD see it, and it displease Him,
and He turn away His wrath from him.
PROVERBS 24:17–18

Okay, so your enemy doesn't repent despite your continued kindness. You leave him in God's hands and sure enough, the day of retribution finally arrives. You hear he's injured in an accident or is about to declare bankruptcy. Whatever you do, do not gloat. Do not rejoice. You're supposed to *love* him, remember?

Keep your fingers completely out of God's wheels of justice. The day He finally brings retribution on your enemy, God will be watching *your* heart and your reactions closely.

73

It pays to start the day with prayer.

To You I have cried out, O LORD, and in the morning my prayer comes before You.
PSALM 88:13

From the moment we wake up, we're already mulling yesterday's unresolved problems and trying to solve them. And we're faithful to jumpstart our brain with a cup of coffee. (We need to, right?)

And yes, we discuss the day's business with coworkers. (To get on top of things.)

But if we *really* want to hit the ground running, we simply must set aside some time every morning to pray. If we take the time to commit our day to God, it will make such a difference!

74

Faithful, daily prayer is vital.

He sought God. . .and as long as he sought the LORD,
God made him prosper.
2 CHRONICLES 26:5

Uzziah became king of Judah after an
invasion and financial calamity. He brought
Judah up from the ashes of defeat and made it
even stronger than before. He reigned for fifty-
two years. God blessed him and prospered him
mightily because Uzziah was in the habit of
praying about things. He was constantly seeking
God.

This same principle still works today.
Faithfully praying about our problems won't
immediately banish them, but God will work *for*
and *with* us and give us victory over things we
face.

75

We must meditate on God.

And Isaac went out to meditate in the field in the evening.
GENESIS 24:63

Isaac was a wealthy patriarch, head of a sheep- and goat-herding empire in southern Canaan. He daily dealt with the details of a huge "business," and had to be both diplomatic and ready to defend. This involved a lot of thought and decisions. No wonder he took time out.

Like Isaac, let's be in the habit of meditating after the day's work—and take time from our busy schedule to unwind, to enjoy a sunset, and to meditate on God.

76

God wants to answer our prayers.

*Delight yourself also in the LORD, and He shall give you
the desires of your heart.*
PSALM 37:4

We often remind God of this promise when
we want Him to grant our heart's desires.
"After all," we say, "I love God. I delight myself in
Him."

There's another condition, however. Note
the word *also*. The *previous* verse says we must
"trust in the Lord." It's quite simple, really:
when we delight in God, we trust that He knows
what's best, and we are delighted to allow Him to
overrule us if what our hearts desire isn't actually
so good for us.

77

We must pray within God's will.

This is the confidence that we have in Him, that if we ask anything according to His will, He hears us.
1 JOHN 5:14

God will grant us good things so long as those things are within His will. Often, however, we pray for things that aren't what God wants for us. After all—honestly now—if He *did* give us a problem-free life or let us be utterly secure financially, how would we learn to trust Him, turn to Him in prayer, or grow spiritually?

If something is God's will, we can expect Him to answer our prayer—but we must sincerely say, "Your will be done" (Matthew 6:10).

78

We must have faith when we pray.

"Whatever things you ask in prayer, believing, you will receive."
MATTHEW 21:22

Many people pray for something they actually need—which is certainly God's will for them—yet have little faith that He'll actually answer prayer. They pray because, well, praying is "what Christians do."

Often, they don't believe when they pray because they doubt that God has the power to do miracles in this day and age. Or they struggle to believe that He *loves them* enough to give them what they need.

God definitely has the power. And He definitely loves you.

79

When we obey,
God answers prayer.

Whatever we ask we receive from Him,
because we keep His commandments and
do those things that are pleasing in His sight.
1 John 3:22

Sometimes we lack faith that God will answer our prayer because we have this niggling feeling that we're disobeying Him somehow. That "niggling feeling" is God's Spirit speaking to our conscience. We want to ignore it and proceed directly to our prayer requests, but prayer is not just us talking to God. It's two-way communication in a relationship.

Let's listen to God and make things right. When our relationship is restored, He'll be happy to listen to us and give us what we pray for.

80

Jesus constantly prays for us.

*It is Christ who. . .is even at the right hand of God,
who also makes intercession for us.*
ROMANS 8:34

Jesus is now in heaven, seated at the right hand of His Father. But He's not just sitting there, micromanaging the entire universe. His mind is still very much on us, and He constantly intercedes with God on our behalf.

What kinds of things is He requesting for us? Well, while He was on Earth, He said of Simon, "I have prayed for you, that your faith should not fail" (Luke 22:32). So it's a fair guess that He's still most interested in our spiritual welfare.

81

God speaks through the Bible.

*Open my eyes, that I may see wondrous
things from Your law.*
PSALM 119:18

What's the best way to find God's will?
Instead of expecting Him to give you an
outstanding sign or speak in an audible voice,
read your Bible. It *is* God's Word, after all, what
He's already said. When it commands, "Don't
steal," well, that *settles* the matter.

Sometimes you read and reread a chapter,
however, but until God opens your eyes, you don't
see an amazing truth right in front of you—at
least you don't *get* it.

That's why you must pray before reading.

82

We must know what
the Bible says.

*"You are mistaken, not knowing the Scriptures
nor the power of God."*
MATTHEW 22:29

Have you ever looked for the verse, "Don't
rob Peter to pay Paul"? You didn't find it
because it's not in the Bible. Mistakes like that can
be embarrassing, but people make more serious
mistakes by assuming that the Bible backs up their
personal beliefs—when it says nothing of the sort.

We can't afford to be mistaken about
important issues or ignorant of what the
scriptures say. Begin faithful, *daily* Bible reading
today. You'll learn some amazing things about
God!

83

We must not go to mediums.

When they say to you, "Seek those who are mediums. . . ,"
should not a people seek their God?
ISAIAH 8:19

You'd be surprised at how many people who "believe in God" consult a psychic to find out what to do. After all, God is silent *just* when they need to know who to marry or whether to give a loan to their cousin.

Or they sneak a peek at their daily horoscope "just in case." Or they read their fortune cookie and take it quite seriously.

Seek God and wait for Him to show you what to do. The wait is worth it.

84

We must listen to godly counselors.

Without counsel, plans go awry, but in the multitude of counselors they are established.
PROVERBS 15:22

When you pray for God's wisdom, God may give *you* that wisdom. . .or He may give it to someone *else*. So don't try to figure everything out yourself. You need the input that godly men or women can give—especially pastors and older saints who've walked many years with God and know how He deals with people.

Get a second and third and fourth opinion just to be sure. Seek out godly advice. . .and listen to it carefully.

85

God can reveal His will clearly.

Cause me to know the way in which I should walk,
for I lift up my soul to You.
PSALM 143:8

Sometimes you need specific direction, and
though you've read your Bible, no verse
jumped out at you. You've counseled with godly
people, but the best they offer is to pray for you.
Well, that's what *you* should be doing, too!

Sometimes you need to pray desperately for
God to make it plain which way you should turn.
If it's a serious decision, fasting will help you give
the Lord your undivided attention.

If you pray wholeheartedly, God will answer
(Jeremiah 33:3).

86

The Bible commands us to work for a living.

*Work with your own hands, as we commanded you. . .
that you may lack nothing.*
1 THESSALONIANS 4:11–12

It's important that Christians have a strong
work ethic: Doing an honest day's work is a
large part of our Christian witness. After all, most
of us spend much of our waking hours in the
workplace. That's where we're called to live out
our faith.

There's another obvious reason for working
diligently: It pays the bills. Otherwise we end up
doing without, or borrowing to make ends meet.

Working is such an integral part of
Christianity that Paul made it a commandment.

87

God gives us power
to earn money.

*"You shall remember the LORD your God,
for it is He who gives you power to get wealth."*
DEUTERONOMY 8:18

Like so many people today, if the Israelites
acquired riches or prospered, they tended to
pat themselves on the back and give themselves
credit. God warned them against thinking that
their skill or shrewdness had brought them
wealth.

They *had* power to get wealth, true, but where
did that power come from? *God*. We may be the
ones sweating, but God is the one who gives us
marketable skills, supplies us with work, and
causes us to prosper.

88

Wealth can be dangerous.

The cares of this world and the deceitfulness of riches
choke the word, and he becomes unfruitful.
MATTHEW 13:22

Riches can be good if handled responsibly and used for God's kingdom, and many Christians promise that they will do exactly that if *only* God would make them wealthy. But riches are very deceitful and cunning enough to ensnare those who "own" them.

If you acquire wealth, don't transfer your trust from God to your bank account, and don't become preoccupied with material things. Gold and goods are beautiful, yes, but not if they overrun you like weeds and choke out your spiritual life.

89

You must commit plans to God.

Unless the LORD builds the house,
they labor in vain who build it.
PSALM 127:1

When you build a house—or a business, or start any project—it involves a lot of work. But don't forget to include God in your planning, or you'll be doing all that work in vain. Without His blessing, you're basically piling up bricks without cement.

It's not enough to assume that your plans please God because they please you. You must spread your blueprints out before the Almighty and give Him veto power. And if you *do* build, build according to His principles.

90

We must be committed to God.

I have learned both to be full and to be hungry,
both to abound and to suffer need.
PHILIPPIANS 4:12

Many couples vow to be true to their spouse "for rich or for poor," because no one can really predict what your future holds. In lean financial times, people relearn the value of such a commitment. If it remains strong, it can sustain their marriage.

We must also remain committed to the Lord no matter what ups and downs we encounter in life. Whether God has us rich or poor, whether we abound or suffer need, let us determine to remain true to God.

91

Worldly gain is no gain at all.

Godliness with contentment is great gain.
For we brought nothing into this world,
and it is certain we can carry nothing out.
1 TIMOTHY 6:6–7

What makes a man truly rich? Winning the lottery? A lifetime of shrewd investments that deliver huge dividends? Owning a mansion and a yacht? No. After all, when he leaves this world, he can't take those gains into eternity. . . so what actual "gain" are they?

Living close to God, becoming more like Him, and being content with what we have. . . that is *truly* great gain.

Godliness and contentment we *can* take out of this world with us.

92

God owns everything on Earth.

For every beast of the forest is Mine,
and the cattle on a thousand hills.
PSALM 50:10

God owns the entire Earth and every creature on it. We don't have a problem with Him owning the wild beasts—after all, He *created* them. And, moreover, we're not using them. But we find it unsettling that God claims that all domestic cattle are His also. We thought they were *our* property.

But God goes further: He states that our lands are actually His, too. In fact, He tells us that we *ourselves* belong to Him.

And He's right. He is God, after all.

93

God blesses us for giving to Him.

Honor the LORD with. . .the firstfruits of all your increase;
so your barns will be filled with plenty.
PROVERBS 3:9–10

God commanded the Israelites to tithe (give Him 10 percent of) all their earnings. These tithes were used to support God's priests and His place of worship and to care for the poor. Tithing was a way of thanking God for blessing them materially. They didn't "lose" by giving either, because God blessed them more as a result.

Whether you believe Christians today should tithe, or simply give as they're able, the principle is clear: give to God and He will give back to you.

94

God blesses all giving—
great and small.

He who sows sparingly will also reap sparingly,
and he who sows bountifully will also reap bountifully.
2 CORINTHIANS 9:6

This simple farming principle also holds
true in God's kingdom: the Lord not only
blesses you when you give, but He blesses you in
proportion to how much you give. So if you can
afford to give generously, do so. God gives great
dividends! Now, if you only give a little, well,
you'll *still* be blessed. . .just not as greatly.

But remember, if you're going through lean
times, the little you can afford to give counts for
more than a millionaire giving a lot.

95

We must keep our promises.

*Whoever falsely boasts of giving is like clouds
and wind without rain.*
PROVERBS 25:14

Some people are quick to promise that they'll do something—they pledge to give money to a needy cause or volunteer their time to help with a project. But then they don't follow through. They *mean* well, but intentions must translate into deeds—otherwise it's all clouds and wind but no rain on the thirsty land.

Don't make promises carelessly, and don't break your word carelessly either. Carry through on what you say you'll do.

96

God always repays His loans.

He who has pity on the poor lends to the LORD,
and He will pay back what he has given.
PROVERBS 19:17

The Old Testament writers stressed giving to the poor, the helpless, and the destitute. Jesus constantly repeated this theme—and the apostles at Jerusalem urged Paul to "remember the poor" (Galatians 2:10). Remember to help them, that is.

In order to motivate us to give to those who cannot repay us, Proverbs tells us to think of it as a temporary loan to the Lord. God will not default on His loans. He will pay back whatever we give. . .and then some.

97

We should do good deeds.

*Tabitha. . .was full of good works
and charitable deeds which she did.*
ACTS 9:36

Tabitha may not have had much money to give, but she did have a great deal of love, and she gave of her time freely. She was a gifted seamstress and was constantly sewing clothing to give to those who had need.

We all can find ways to do charitable deeds for others. If nothing else, we can offer our hands and our time to help them. Or we can lend a pair of sympathetic ears to the discouraged.

98

Life is often hard for Christians.

*"We must through many tribulations
enter the kingdom of God."*
ACTS 14:22

Some Christians assume that God will so bless
believers that no trouble will ever befall them.
If the early Christians had entertained such a
doctrine, Paul set them straight very quickly. He
went from city to city exhorting them to continue
in the faith and warning, "We'll endure lots of
trials and troubles before we get to heaven." No
sugarcoating the message there!

We, too, will face tough times. Let us
therefore resolve that, come what may, we, too,
will continue to be faithful to God.

99

Hard times won't last forever.

May the God of all grace. . .after you have suffered a
while, perfect, establish, strengthen, and settle you.
1 PETER 5:10

When we're in the middle of suffering, or
enduring trouble that tests our resolve, it's
comforting to know that it won't last forever. God
may allow us to suffer for a while, but it's not His
intention that we do so endlessly. God cares for
us, and He knows our limits.

All suffering that God's people endure serves
a purpose—a *good* purpose, ultimately. And
after the trouble is past, God takes us out of the
furnace, settles us, establishes us, and strengthens
us.

100

Victory comes to those
who persevere.

*Let us not grow weary while doing good, for in due season
we shall reap if we do not lose heart.*
GALATIANS 6:9

It's *wise* to let go of futile ventures and move
on to productive things. But too often, we let
worthy dreams die because we become weary
with a lack of results and give up.

It can be difficult to know which situation
holds true with personal visions or ventures, but
it's never difficult when it comes to Christian
living. We are *never* to stop choosing right over
wrong or doing good to others.

It may take a while, but we will always reap a
reward.

101

God gets good out of bad situations.

We know that all things work together
for good to those who love God.
ROMANS 8:28

This verse *isn't* saying that all things that happen to Christians are good. Some things are detrimental or just plain wrong, and shouldn't have happened.

But God is loving and powerful, and He is in the business of redeeming lives and situations. He can make all experiences—including negative ones—*work together* for His purposes so that good comes from them in the end.

Not always in this life, but certainly in the next, all tears will be wiped away and all wrongs righted.

102

God corrects and trains us.

"Behold, happy is the man whom God corrects;
therefore do not despise the chastening of the Almighty."
JOB 5:17

We often like to think we're doing pretty much okay and have no need of major correction, thank you very much. We're not happy, therefore, when God sends sickness or complications or financial reversals into our lives. "O God! Why are you punishing me?" we cry. (What we often mean is, "Why me?")

Cheer up! It's not punishment. It's God disciplining us. We're His sons and daughters, and He loves us enough to correct us. That thought ought to make us happy.

103

We must not give in to despair.

We are hard-pressed on every side, yet not crushed;
we are perplexed, but not in despair.
2 CORINTHIANS 4:8

Even the "great" apostle Paul confessed that he felt the stress at times. Pressure was bearing down on him from every side till he felt like he'd be crushed under the strain—but he *wasn't* crushed. And there were days when he was perplexed. He either didn't know why God had allowed something to happen, or he had no idea what he should do—but he didn't give in to despair.

He just kept trusting God and praying till his circumstances changed.

104

We need friends
and to be friends.

God, who comforts the downcast,
comforted us by the coming of Titus.
2 CORINTHIANS 7:6

When Paul was in Macedonia, there was trouble all around. He admitted that he felt fear. He was exhausted. Paul could take a lot, but he was only human. He got to where he was downcast, and the Greek word used here means "depressed."

God *Himself* comforts the downcast, but He also uses people. This time He sent Paul's close friend Titus to encourage him. May we be that kind of friend to others, and may we be open to receiving comfort when we're down.

105

Fear is not from God.

God has not given us a spirit of fear,
but of power and of love and of a sound mind.
2 TIMOTHY 1:7

When we become Christians, God's Spirit
enters and begins to transform our lives.
Now, if we feel gripped by fear, we need to realize
that God is not the one giving us that fear. (Fear is
not one of the gifts of the Spirit.)

We should reject such fear and overcome it
by reminding ourselves that the Holy Spirit gives
us *good* and *empowering* gifts like love, power, and
a sound mind. Claim these God-given gifts, and
they will displace fear.

106

Faith can conquer fear.

"Why are you so fearful?
How is it that you have no faith?"
MARK 4:40

When you're nearly overwhelmed by troubles or danger, there seems to be good reason to fear. The twelve disciples in the storm-tossed, wave-washed boat certainly thought so!

What Jesus asked was not, "Why are you afraid *at all*?" but, "Why are you *so full of fear*?" The boat was still bearing up, but their minds were already swamped and sinking—to the point where they had no faith left.

It may require a terrific effort of will, but we must face and overcome fear with faith.

107

Love kicks fear out the door.

*There is no fear in love; but perfect love casts out fear. . .
he who fears has not been made perfect in love.*
1 JOHN 4:18

Most of us understand how faith can overcome fear. After all, faith is a powerful force, the opposite of fear—which results from a *lack* of faith. But how, we ask, can something as "sweet and gentle" as *love* thrust out fear?

Well, God *is* love and God is all-powerful. He is the Light that pushes back the darkness. A person who is "perfect in love" is so full of God's Spirit that there's little room left for darkness, doubt, and fear.

108

Trust helps you sleep.

When you lie down, you will not be afraid;
yes, you will lie down and your sleep will be sweet.
PROVERBS 3:24

Perhaps when you lie down at night you can barely fall asleep. You're not afraid of a monster under your bed—haven't been for years. You're not living in a war-wracked city either. So what has you afraid? Bills, your kids, your marriage, the economy, the future. . . Call it worry, but if it's stressing you so badly you can't sleep, it's fear.

God wants you to be well-rested. So pray—hand your problems off to God and trust Him to take care of things. Then have sweet dreams.

109

We must resist the devil.

Submit to God. Resist the devil and he will flee from you.
Draw near to God and He will draw near to you.
JAMES 4:7–8

Resisting the devil involves more than just commanding him in Jesus' name to leave—though that's certainly a necessary step. The key to resisting Satan is found in the two other admonitions: "draw near to God" and "submit to God."

When we're close to God we experience more of His power. When we submit to God's will instead of resisting Him, the devil no longer has a toehold.

Kneeling before God enables us to stand up to Satan. And he *will* flee.

110

God's Word helps us overcome evil.

The word of God abides in you,
and you have overcome the wicked one.
1 JOHN 2:14

When Jesus was fasting and the devil repeatedly tried to tempt him to sin, Jesus quoted the Word of God to refute him. Again and again, Jesus replied, "It is written. . ." then quoted a passage that exposed the devil's lie. We need to do the same.

That's where it really pays to know what the Bible says.

Of course, we need to *obey* those verses, not merely memorize them like lines from a theatrical production. Then we can speak the Word of God with authority.

111

Satan constantly fights God's will.

*We wanted to come to you—even I, Paul, time and
again—but Satan hindered us.*
1 Thessalonians 2:18

Have you ever tried to do something for God
and found yourself fighting through delays
and roadblocks every foot of the way? "Why?"
you ask.

This happened to the apostle Paul, too. Satan
constantly fights God's will. (No surprise there.)

Again and again, the devil hindered Paul
from visiting the Christians in Thessalonica.
Satan wanted to stop him, or if nothing else, to
slow him down.

If that happens to you, don't give up. Pray for
God to drive off the devil and push on through.

112

Spending time with God gives us strength.

But those who wait on the LORD shall renew their strength.
ISAIAH 40:31

Everyone runs out of strength at some point. Even youths with seemingly boundless physical energy eventually stop bounding. And all of us reach points where our mental stamina wears out and our spiritual power flickers.

How do we renew our mental and spiritual strength? By spending time with God and allowing Him to recharge our batteries. It takes a while, we have to wait on Him, but if we want to keep going, we have to set aside that time.

It is *so* worth it!

113

God upholds the fallen.

Though he fall, he shall not be utterly cast down;
for the LORD upholds him with His hand.
PSALM 37:24

You've seen that man or woman: They're struggling in hard times. They're battered this way and that till they weaken. . .and then they fall. They're worn out, or some temptation takes them down. Perhaps you've been there yourself.

But somehow they get back up. They've been cast down but not utterly cast down, because something caught them. That something was the Lord. Never forget that "underneath are the everlasting arms" (Deuteronomy 33:27).

God's mighty hand upholds the fallen and enables them to rise again.

114

Happiness strengthens us.

"Do not sorrow, for the joy of the LORD is your strength."
NEHEMIAH 8:10

It's right to mourn and weep when we realize
how far we've strayed and disobeyed God.
That's what the Jews in Nehemiah's day did.
But there's also a time to receive His forgiveness
and rejoice. It's not God's will for us to
flagellate ourselves, to continually mope around
discouraged and defeated.

Yes, God has forgiven our sins! Yes, He still
loves us! Yes, He gives us fresh mercy! Knowing
these things should give us joy. That joy then gives
us strength to face life.

115

Jesus has power to heal.

*Jesus went about. . .healing all kinds of sickness
and all kinds of disease among the people.*
MATTHEW 4:23

While He was on Earth, Jesus was constantly
healing sicknesses and diseases. From
morning till evening, the sick came to Him, and
Jesus healed them all. It was a clear way to show
that He *loved* them. It was also proof that He was
the Son of God.

Thank God for good doctors and effective
medicines these days. They help many people.
But Jesus *still* loves us, and He's *still* the Son of
God and *still* has the power to heal—so don't
forget to pray.

116

Being sick is sometimes a good thing.

*It is good for me that I have been afflicted,
that I may learn Your statutes.*
PSALM 119:71

If Jesus can heal, why, we ask, doesn't He always heal us when *we're* sick? Well, perhaps we don't have the faith that He can do the miracle. But there's also another reason. . . .

Sometimes it's actually good for us to have a handicap or suffer sickness. Paul had to have a "thorn in the flesh" (apparently an eye disease) to keep him humble. Other times, God allows us to become sick to get our attention and speak to us about things we've been ignoring.

117

God helps the desperate and the distressed.

You have been a strength to the poor, a strength to the needy in his distress, a refuge from the storm.
ISAIAH 25:4

When we're passing through a dark valley, we often feel abandoned by God: We cry out to Him but hear no answer. We weep that we can't bear up under the strain and beg Him to deliver us. . .but no answer. We pray for protection from the tempest. . .but still no answer.

And yet we pass through our deep distress. We realize that God has, after all, given us the strength to carry our load. The storm passes and we are still standing.

118

God delivers those
who trust Him.

He shall deliver them from the wicked,
and save them, because they trust in Him.
PSALM 37:40

There may come a time in your life when a truly wicked person determines to bring you to ruin—and there may seem to be little you can do to stop him or her. What do you do? What *can* you do?

You must pray to God to save you. And no matter how grim or threatening the circumstances seem, you must never stop trusting that God has the *power* to protect you, and that He *will* protect you. And He will.

119

God disposes of the wicked.

*God will rebuke them and they will flee far away. . .
like a rolling thing before the whirlwind.*
ISAIAH 17:13

Your enemies may be rooted in secure positions of power, but God is far, far more powerful. He can suddenly rise up in His fury like a windstorm in the desert, tear the wicked up by the roots, and send them rolling and bouncing powerlessly along. He thrusts them along like tumbleweed. . .till they are gone.

Living through a desert storm is an awe-inspiring experience, but more terrifying still is to see God rebuke the wicked with the force of a whirlwind.

120

God foils the crafty.

He frustrates the devices of the crafty,
so that their hands cannot carry out their plans.
JOB 5:12

Prayer moves the hand of God, and in a world increasingly filled with con artists, hackers, and identity thieves, we certainly need to pray for God's protection. Those who wish to defraud us think they're so clever, but God is even cleverer. He can stymie their efforts and cause everything to go so haywire that they can't carry out their plans. They won't even be able to set a mousetrap properly.

We can't confound and confuse the crafty like that, but we *can* pray.

121

God's angels protect us.

He shall give His angels charge over you,
to keep you in all your ways.
PSALM 91:11

Many people believe that God assigns a guardian angel to protect us from the day we're born till the day we die. Some insist that we have *two* angels constantly guarding us, one on each hand. The Bible doesn't tell us the details, but we can be sure of this: angels *do* watch over us.

God gives them charge over us. To be "given charge" doesn't mean that they boss us around; it means that they're commanded to watch out for us.

That's a comforting thought.

122

God protects us every day.

Through the LORD's mercies we are not consumed, because His compassions fail not. They are new every morning.
LAMENTATIONS 3:22–23

So many things can go wrong every day, and we are like toddlers, almost daily stumbling between hot stoves and medicine cabinets. Accidents and troubles would surely swallow us up if it weren't for the Lord's mercy. His compassion just never peters out.

This isn't to say that God protects us from all harm or shields us from every consequence of our carelessness—but the fact that we're still here is proof that He hasn't allowed them to *consume* us.

123

God can do absolutely anything.

*"Behold, I am the LORD, the God of all flesh.
Is there anything too hard for Me?"*
JEREMIAH 32:27

That is the question, isn't it? And the answer, in the same chapter, is, "You have made the heavens and the earth by Your great power. . . . There is nothing too hard for you" (Jeremiah 32:17).

God not only created all life on Earth, but the Earth itself. In fact, He made the entire universe of which the Earth is a very small part. A God with *that* much power would hardly find our problems too difficult.

We need to remind ourselves of that occasionally.

124

God can do what we can't.

"With men this is impossible,
but with God all things are possible."
MATTHEW 19:26

When problems come our way, our first reaction is usually to try to solve it—which is a good thing. God has given us problem-solving brains for that very purpose. But some problems are simply too difficult to resolve. Even bringing in the experts won't help.

It's frustrating to realize that we're in an impossible situation, but fortunately, there's a miracle worker who can help us—God. He has unlimited power. He can do literally anything.

So don't wait too long before you call Him.

125

God makes weak people strong.

When I am weak, then I am strong.
2 CORINTHIANS 12:10

Jesus taught many conundrums that turn conventional human wisdom on its head: "The first shall be last. . . . Bless those who curse you. . . . He that loses his life saves it. . . . The weak are strong." Odd statements. . .yet, amazingly, they *work.*

The reason these "upside-down" principles work is because they factor God into the equation. When we're weak and trusting, God's power rests on us. That makes us strong—*far* stronger than we'd be if we depended only on our strength.

126

God doesn't need big armies.

*"Nothing restrains the LORD from saving
by many or by few."*
1 SAMUEL 14:6

When God parted the Red Sea and defeated the Egyptians, He didn't need any help. Moses basically said, "Stand back and watch God save us!" (Exodus 14:13).

Yet when God says that He *does* want people involved, we suddenly get the idea that He needs a *lot* of us—a regular army, in fact. Not so. God might use many people to save the day, or He might use only a few.

Never forget that though God is *one*, He counts for "many."

127

We should witness to others.

*"Go into all the world and preach
the gospel to every creature."*
MARK 16:15

When Jesus gave this command two
thousand years ago, Christians headed out,
preaching the Gospel. They were not only living
examples of what a follower of Christ should be,
but they spoke up and *told* others about Jesus.

This command didn't just apply to the apostles
who heard Jesus say it—all Christians back then
preached the Gospel. And it's not only for pastors
and evangelists today—it's for all of us.

The world still needs to hear about Jesus, so
let's tell them!

128

There's no need to be ashamed of Jesus.

I am not ashamed of the gospel of Christ, for it is the power of God to salvation for everyone who believes.
ROMANS 1:16

Many of us genuinely love Jesus, understand that only He can save us, yet we don't talk to others about Him. We say that we're shy. We're ashamed of being labeled a religious nut. We don't like being preachy or pushy.

So let's *not* be pushy or preachy. And if we speak gently and not wild-eyed, we'll avoid being labeled a fanatic. We must believe that people *need* salvation then pray for God to make opportunities for us to speak to them. . .gently.

129

We must know what we believe.

Always be ready to give a defense to everyone who asks you a reason for the hope that is in you.
1 PETER 3:15

Some people, when they learn that you're a Christian, will ask *why* you believe there's a God, why you have faith in Jesus, why you have hope of eternal life, etc. Whether they're asking sincerely or skeptically, you must be prepared to give them a reason why you believe.

You don't have to give complicated answers, but you should know your Bible well enough to give an intelligent answer with sincerity. It also helps to read books that explain and defend the Christian faith.

130

You're bound to have enemies.

*All who desire to live godly in Christ Jesus
will suffer persecution.*
2 TIMOTHY 3:12

It seems like many Christians go through
their entire lives without ever experiencing
persecution, but persecution doesn't just mean
being beaten or driven from town—as happens
in some countries. It also means being lied about,
maligned, and opposed.

Many a peaceful Christian who has taken
a stand for godly values and resisted pressure to
back down, has been surprised at how suddenly
persecution can arise—even from former friends.

Don't be surprised. Jesus was persecuted, and
we will be, too, if we follow Him.

131

Be glad if you're persecuted.

"Blessed are you when they revile and persecute you. . .
for My sake."
MATTHEW 5:11

When you obey Jesus' commands and do what's right, and foul-mouthed people revile (curse) you for it, the experience can be unpleasant and embarrassing. . .even intimidating. Of course, that's the effect they're trying to achieve.

But don't let it get to you. Jesus says you're blessed when people curse you and treat you badly. You're so blessed, in fact, that you should rejoice! Why? Because God will richly compensate you in heaven for everything you suffer for His sake.

That's a promise!

132

We can endure hostility.

Consider Him who endured such hostility from sinners
against Himself, lest you become weary
and discouraged in your souls.
HEBREWS 12:3

Knowing that you'll be rewarded in heaven
for suffering persecution here on Earth
is a great encouragement. However, if the
opposition goes on and on, even promises of
heavenly rewards can seem distant. So how do
you endure prolonged hostility without becoming
discouraged?

Look to Jesus. Consider how much God's own
Son suffered—*years* of hostile opposition from
His enemies, lies, attacks on His reputation—and
finally beatings, mockery, and crucifixion.

You haven't suffered that much, so take heart.

133

We can defeat ignorant, foolish men.

This is the will of God, that by doing good you may put to silence the ignorance of foolish men.
1 PETER 2:15

Many people today have skewed, unfavorable opinions about Christianity. Some have had unpleasant encounters with Christians, true, but many get their views from biased media reports or the constant disparaging remarks made by vocal unbelievers. The Bible calls this "the ignorance of foolish men."

God also tells us how to *dispel* this ignorance: we are to live exemplary lives, be honest in business, obey the law, and do good. If we do this consistently, people will eventually realize that Christianity is a good thing.

134

We must remember persecuted Christians.

Remember the prisoners as if chained with them—
those who are mistreated—since you yourselves
are in the body also.
HEBREWS 13:3

In America, we usually don't suffer serious persecution for our faith, but Christians in many nations suffer terribly. They're mistreated, attacked, imprisoned, tortured, and killed. We must not become so settled in our good life—or absorbed by our problems—that we forget them. We must feel their pain as if chained right beside them.

If we can help persecuted Christians, we should. Many churches even sponsor suffering believers as refugees.

Most of all, however, we must remember them in prayer.

135

Judgment is slow for a reason.

"You are a gracious and merciful God,
slow to anger and abundant in lovingkindness,
One who relents from doing harm."
JONAH 4:2

When people threaten us, we wonder, "What's God waiting for? Why doesn't He judge them. . .*now*?" Jonah wondered that same thing. The Assyrians were militaristic, oppressive, and cruel, yet just when God was poised to destroy their capital, Nineveh, they repented. So God postponed judgment.

A very frustrated Jonah knew why: God loved the Assyrians, and He longed to show even them mercy. Fortunately for the people of the world, God is more merciful than we are.

136

God doesn't go by our schedule.

*Though it tarries, wait for it; because it will surely come,
it will not tarry.*
HABAKKUK 2:3

God has made many promises in His Word—
promises to bless us if we obey Him, and
to answer our prayers. Yet many times it appears
that God isn't doing anything. . .and we despair.

We're so impatient. We expect God's train
to come in on our schedule, and when it doesn't,
we think He's late. We don't want to wait one
more moment. Yet, if God takes a little longer
than we'd anticipated, it does us good to continue
to trust and to wait. The time will come when
God *will* act.

137

It's worth waiting for God.

*My soul waits for the Lord more than
those who watch for the morning.*
PSALM 130:6

In ancient days, soldiers stood atop city walls
by night on guard duty. They were cold and
had to be constantly vigilant, so they longed for
sunrise when the danger was past and their shift
ended.

When we spend long months praying and
waiting, and God finally answers, it's like the sun
rising over the dark hills. We knew that God *would*
eventually answer. It just took time for the day to
arrive.

Keep on watching and waiting no matter how
dark it is. Sunrise is coming!

138

God can be trusted completely.

Trust in the LORD with all your heart,
and lean not on your own understanding.
PROVERBS 3:5

God's ways are so much higher than our ways. We're like children learning basic addition and subtraction, compared to a college professor teaching advanced formulas that fill entire blackboards. Yet we insist that all life should be as simple as $1 + 1 = 2$.

We can't possibly understand how God's ways work or how He gets the results that He does. We're way out of our depth. We just have to place our hand in His, trust that He knows what He's doing, and obey Him.

139

Give God all your worries.

Casting all your care upon Him, for He cares for you.
1 PETER 5:7

When Peter says "care" he means anxious thoughts. Some of us worry about every little thing. Others of us don't sweat the small stuff; no, we only get frantic about middle-sized problems and big problems.

But whatever problems arise to harass us, the Bible tells us to heave them into God's hands. They'll just wear us down and wear us out if we try to carry them.

We can trust God to bear our concerns. After all, He loves us. He cares for us.

140

God removes our anxiety.

Be anxious for nothing, but. . .
let your requests be made known to God.
PHILIPPIANS 4:6

When Paul says, "Be anxious for nothing," it's understood that there *are* situations that you should be concerned about. The question is what you do about them. Do you just think and think about them until your mind's spinning like a hamster on a treadmill? Or do you turn that concern into a prayer and ask God to help you?

If you earnestly pray, the Lord will answer. Then He promises, "the peace of God. . .will guard your hearts and minds" (verse 7).

141

God wants us to have fun.

A feast is made for laughter.
ECCLESIASTES 10:19

While we must take our faith seriously, there are times when we need to lighten up and have a good laugh. A family feast where we enjoy good food and good company is literally *made* for laughter. And so were we.

When the Prodigal Son returned, his overjoyed father threw a party, and everyone enjoyed the festivities. Only the overly serious older brother was angry at the "waste" and refused to join in.

Remember: God wants us to enjoy family, friends, food, and fun!

142

It's healthy to be happy.

A merry heart does good, like medicine.
PROVERBS 17:22

People have known for thousands of years that being happy and laughing was a good thing. It didn't take a lot of thought to come to that conclusion. But the Bible took it a step further, stating that merriment literally had the power to heal just like medicine.

Sure enough, in recent years clinical tests have shown that laughter reduces stress hormones, increases pain tolerance, strengthens the immune system, and increases the level of health-enhancing endorphins. All good stuff.

143

We can be happy in hard times.

You greatly rejoice, though now for a little while,
if need be, you have been grieved by various trials.
1 PETER 1:6

Perhaps you're thinking, "I'd like to be happy, but I'm really going through a rough time now." Sorrow is the right reaction at times, and is actually necessary, but it's possible to sorrow too deep and too long. We can become "swallowed up with too much sorrow" (2 Corinthians 2:7). We must remember to rejoice.

Think of the joy you'll one day enjoy, eternally, in heaven. Really *believe* that it will happen one day, and you can't help but rejoice in the midst of your grieving.

144

This world will end.

*Behold, He is coming with clouds. . .and all the tribes of
the earth will mourn because of Him.*
REVELATION 1:7

Jesus is coming again just as He promised
He would! And when He returns, the world
as we now know it will come to an end. It will
not be a happy day for the unsaved who've been
persecuting Christians. They'll mourn when
they see Jesus because they'll realize that we were
telling them the truth. . .only now it's too late.

It will be a very *happy* day for Christians,
however. The day man's rule over this world ends,
Heaven on Earth begins.

145

We'll be transformed at the Rapture.

We also eagerly wait for the Savior, the Lord Jesus Christ, who will transform our lowly body.
PHILIPPIANS 3:20–21

We long for Jesus to come back. Not only will He end all wars, bring justice on Earth, feed the hungry, and restore the world to its original paradisiacal state. . .but He will miraculously transform our physical bodies.

No longer will we be weak, sick, aging, and mortal. We will be powerful, glorious, forever young, and immortal! We will be completely changed—with no more pain, suffering, and disease. . .ever again.

No wonder we eagerly await Jesus' Second Coming!

146

Jesus will judge Christians.

We must all appear before the judgment seat of Christ,
that each one may receive the things done in the body.
2 CORINTHIANS 5:10

One day, all Christians will appear before
Jesus to account for what they have done
with their lives. But the Judgment Seat of Christ
is different from the judgment of the world when
the wicked are condemned. Those who appear
before Christ at this time are saved.

It will be a time of great rejoicing as Jesus
richly rewards Christians for every good deed
they have done, every loving word they have ever
spoken, and every bit of suffering they endured
for His name.

147

Bad deeds will be burned up.

If anyone's work is burned, he will suffer loss; but he himself will be saved, yet so as through fire.
1 CORINTHIANS 3:15

Jesus will reward Christians for the good they've done. . .but what about their *bad* deeds—their selfish attitudes, the time wasted, their sins? Jesus took the punishment for sin on the cross, so we know that's taken care of.

All of their bad deeds will be utterly burned up. They themselves will be saved, but will "suffer loss" because they'll receive no reward for those wasted portions of their life.

Only their good works will enter with them into eternity.

148

Happy days are coming to stay.

"God will wipe away every tear from their eyes; there shall
be no more death, nor sorrow, nor crying."
REVELATION 21:4

Many Christians believe that when we realize the ways we failed to live for Christ, we'll weep. . .that these are the tears that God will wipe away. That's part of it.

But there's a deeper meaning here: we try our best to live for Christ in this world but are often beset by sickness, financial lack, the death of loved ones, suffering, and persecution for Jesus' sake. All these sad things will one day end.

We'll weep no longer in heaven—just enjoy endless happiness.

149

You'll have your day in the sun.

Then the righteous will shine forth as the sun in the kingdom of their Father.
MATTHEW 13:43

Jesus said that the poor and the meek (the humble) are blessed, for they shall inherit the kingdom of heaven (Matthew 5:3, 5). They don't *seem* too blessed at the moment: they're weak, and the mighty of this world overlook them and tread them underfoot. But the day is coming when the righteous will reign with Christ, and *no one* will be able to overlook them.

When God's kingdom comes, and He rewards those who love Him, they'll blaze with glory like the sun!

150

Heaven is unimaginably wonderful.

"Eye has not seen, nor ear heard, nor have entered into the heart of man, the things which God has prepared for those who love Him."
1 CORINTHIANS 2:9

Paul penned this line in AD 55 and at the time, Christians had very little idea what heaven was like, or how wonderful it was. Certainly no one had been there and returned to write about it in any detail—not till AD 95, that is, when John was transported into the heavenlies and wrote the book of Revelation.

Of course, not even John's breathtaking description truly does heaven justice. As the saying goes, "You had to have *been* there!"

One day you *will* be there.

Scripture Index